HOW THINGS WORK

CRANES DUMP TRUCKS BULLDOZERS

AND OTHER
BUILDING
MACHINES

TERRY JENNINGS

Kingfisher Books

NEW YORK

KINGFISHER
Larousse Kingfisher Chambers Inc.
95 Madison Avenue
New York, New York 10016

First edition 1993
6 8 10 9 7 (PB)
2 4 6 8 10 9 7 5 3 1 (HC)
2 4 6 8 10 9 7 5 3 1 (RLB)
Copyright © Grisewood & Dempsey Ltd. 1992

Library of Congress Cataloging-in-Publication Data
Jennings, Terry J.
Cranes, dump trucks, bulldozers & other building machines
Terry Jennings. — 1st American ed.
p.cm. (How things work) Includes index.
Summary: Investigates, in text and labelled diagrams and
illustrations, the functions of various kinds of building machines
and how they work. Includes instructions for related projects
and experiments
1. Construction equipment—Juvenile literature.
[1. Construction equipment. 2. Machinery.]
I. Title. II. Series: How things work.
TH900.J46 1993
690-dc20 92-23370 CIP AC

ISBN 1-85697-866-4 (HC)
ISBN 1-85697-865-6 (PB)
ISBN 1-85697-657-2 (RLB)

Printed in Hong Kong

Series editor: Jackie Gaff
Series designer: David West Children's Books
Author: Terry Jennings
Text contributors: Jacqui Bailey, Jackie Gaff, Chris Maynard
Consultant: Robert C. McWilliam (The Science Museum)
Cover illustration: Micheal Fisher (Garden Studio)
Illustrators: Darren Fletcher pp. 32-3, Chris Forsey pp. 6-7,
(insets 10-11), 16-21, 38-9; Hayward Art Group pp. 10-11,
14-15, 28-9; Simon Tegg pp. 8-9, 12-13, 22-7, 36-7;
Ian Thompson pp. 2-5, 30-1, 34-5.
Research: A.R. Blann

The publishers would like to thank: Benford Construction
Equipment Manufacturers; Blaw-Knox Construction
Equipment Corporation (Mr. David Wetjen); Grayston White
& Sparrow Ltd.; Ingersoll-Rand Sales Company Ltd.;
J.C. Bamford Excavators Ltd. (Mr. Tony Fellows); Liebherr
(Great Britain) Ltd.; H. Leverton Ltd.; Marubeni-Komatsu Ltd.;
NCK Ltd.; Perkins Engines.

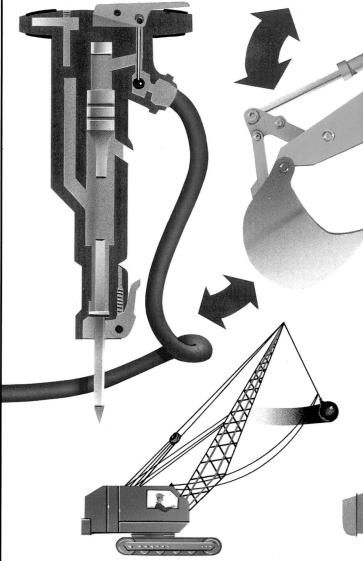

CONTENTS

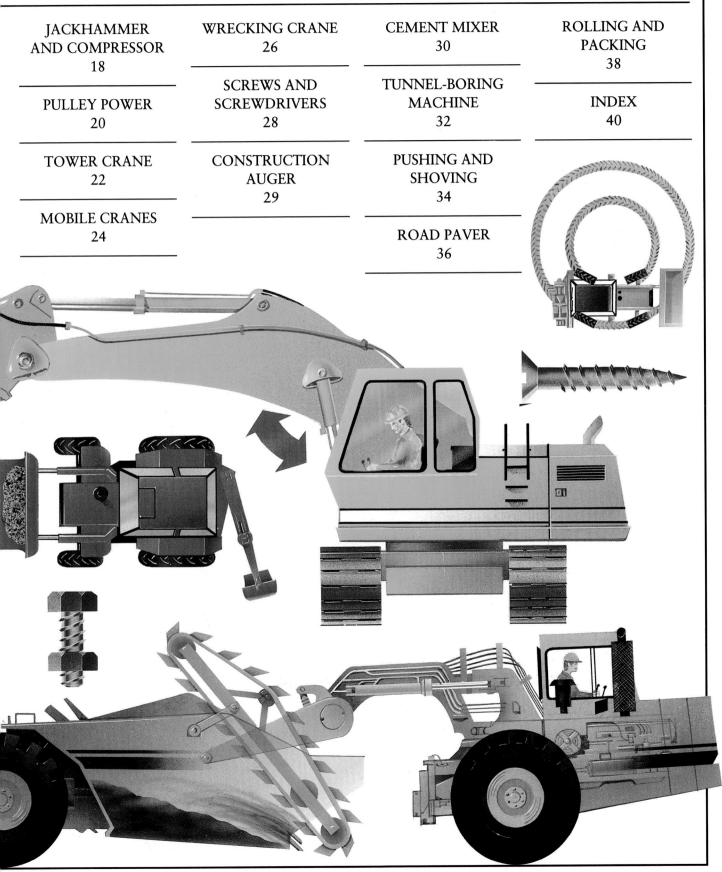

FAMOUS BUILDING FIRSTS

Fossils of stone tools have been found near the bones of *Homo habilis* ("handy man"), the earliest human species. *Homo habilis* lived in East Africa nearly 2 million years ago.

△ By 3000 B.C., the Egyptians were using copper saws. By 850 B.C., they were using iron saws to cut stone.

No one knows exactly when pulleys or cranes were invented, but the Assyrians are thought to have been using a simple rope and pulley system by about 1500 B.C.

△ In the 1st century B.C., the Roman architect and engineer Vitruvius published the first description of a crane, in his work *De architectura*. From Roman times on, cranes were often powered by human treadmills.

△ By A.D. 200, the wheelbarrow was being used in China. It wasn't known in Europe until the 1100s.

In the 1400s, the first metal screws and bolts appeared. Wood screws were first used around 1550, but the screwdriver wasn't invented until after the 1740s!

▽ In about 1480, the Italian artist and inventor Leonardo da Vinci designed the first pivoting (revolving) crane.

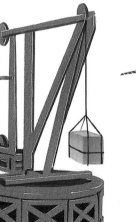

In 1796, a hydraulic ram using the pressure of water was invented by the Montgolfier brothers of France .

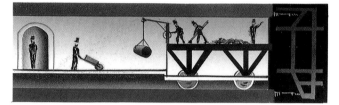

△ In 1818, French-born engineer Marc Isambard Brunel patented the first tunneling shield. It was used on a tunnel under the river Thames in London.

In 1859, the steam roller was invented by Louis Lemoine of France.

In 1861, the pneumatic drill was invented by the French engineer Germain Sommeiller, and used in constructing the Mont Cenis Tunnel through the Alps.

△ In 1895, the first electric hand drill was built by the German Wilhelm Fein. (Its forerunner, the awl, existed in prehistoric times.)

In 1904, in the U.S., Benjamin Holt invented crawler tracks. They were first used on a tractor in 1908.

In 1917, S. Duncan Black and Alonso G. Decker of the U.S. made the first electric drill with an on-off switch.

△ In the 1920s, truck-mounted cranes and cement mixers appeared. Bulldozers were developed at this time too, from crawler tractors.

In 1974, the Sears Tower was finished in Chicago. At 1,454 ft. (443 m), it is still the world's tallest building today.

INTRODUCTION

The great stone circles of Stonehenge, on Salisbury Plain in England, are a remarkable example of ancient building skills.

The earliest work on the site dates from about 2500 B.C. It was completed around 1500 B.C., when 80 huge stones, each weighing an average of 26 tons, were erected by levers and muscle power.

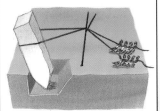

Archaeologists think that each stone was rolled to the edge of an oblong hole which had a sloping ramp on one side. The stone was levered into the hole and then pulled and levered upright.

The first person ever to use a stone ax to cut down a tree made as much use of a building machine as the driver of the biggest bulldozer in operation today. A machine is something that allows work to be done more easily or quickly, so the simple stone tools of prehistoric peoples were as useful to them as today's range of complex machinery is to us.

In some ways, modern building machines are not as complex as they may seem. As you will discover in this book, even the biggest is based on one of five simple machines — the lever, the wheel and axle, the pulley, the ramp, and the screw — and all these machines were invented thousands of years ago.

The most important change that has taken place over the centuries is in the way machines are powered. Until the invention of the steam engine in the 1700s, people had to rely on the power of their own muscles, or on animal, wind, or water power. It is amazing to think that all the great monuments of the past — the Egyptian pyramids, Roman bridges and aqueducts, the great medieval cathedrals — were built with only simple machines and muscle power!

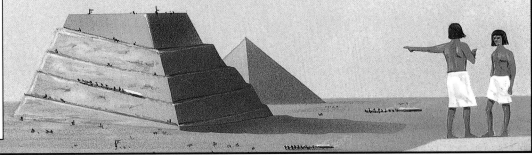

LEVERS – SHIFTING THE LOAD

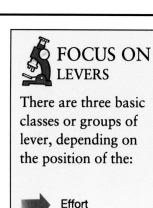

FOCUS ON LEVERS

There are three basic classes or groups of lever, depending on the position of the:

➡ Effort

➡ Load

▲ Fulcrum

1st class levers
Fulcrum is between effort and load

2nd class levers
Load is between effort and fulcrum

3rd class levers
Effort is between fulcrum and load

Levers are the simplest of all machines, but they are among the most useful. They make it easier to move things because they magnify the effort put into a job, changing a small force into a large force.

All levers involve three things. The effort is the work put into the job — such as lifting, pulling, or turning — the fulcrum is the place where the lever pivots or turns, and the load is the thing you want to move.

☐ CROWBAR
1st CLASS LEVER

Quite a small effort pushing down on the crowbar handle is turned into a large upward force to raise the rock (the load). The small rock acts as the fulcrum here.

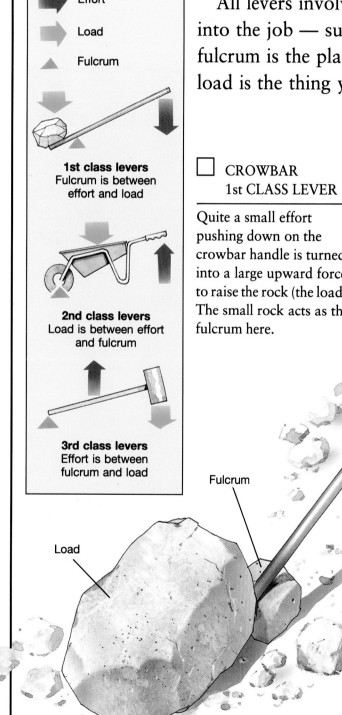

Fulcrum

Load

☐ WHEELBARROW
2nd CLASS LEVER

Pulling up the wheel-barrow handles is quite a small effort which allows you to lift heavy loads balanced behind the wheel (the fulcrum).

TEST IT OUT!

The longer a lever is, and the closer the fulcrum is to the object, the easier it is to move the object. Test this out by resting a heavy book on the first inch of a 12-inch (30-cm) ruler. Slide a pencil (the fulcrum) under the ruler's 8-inch (20-cm) mark and use one finger to press down on the ruler end. Now move the pencil to the 4-inch (10-cm) mark and press down on the ruler again — it should be easier to raise the book now!

Fulcrum

☐ HAMMER 3rd CLASS LEVER

The hammer acts as a lever when it is used to hit the chisel down to break the rock. Here, the effort is lifting the hammer. The fulcrum is in the worker's shoulder joints, and the load is the hammer head.

☐ ALL SORTS OF LEVERS

There are hundreds of different levers. Many of the things you use every day are levers.

1st class lever
Spoon to lift lid

2nd class lever
Bottle opener

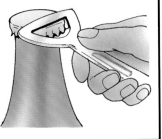

FOCUS ON ARCHIMEDES

Archimedes was a famous Greek mathematician and inventor who was born in about 287 B.C. (nearly 2,300 years ago). He is supposed to have said this about levers:

"Give me a place to stand and I will move the Earth."

To try this he would have had to stand out in space! But it still would have been impossible, because even today we can't make strong enough levers and fulcrums.

Excavators are machines that dig holes by scooping up and lifting out buckets of soil and rock. They are designed so that levers help them to do this heavy work. In size, excavators range from small machines that are used for ditch clearing, to large ones that can lift and dump as much as 20 tons of rock at one time. The depth of the hole the excavator digs depends on the length of the dipper arm and boom. The machine illustrated here can dig a hole over 16 feet (5 m) deep and lift a load weighing more than 1 ton.

□ DIPPER ARM

The dipper arm works as a 1st class lever, with the fulcrum between the effort and the load. The hinged joint between the boom and the dipper arm is the fulcrum. The load is the bucketful of soil or rocks.

Hydraulic ram

Joint

□ HYDRAULIC RAMS

Hydraulic rams (see pages 10-11) slide in and out to make the boom, the dipper arm, and the bucket move.

□ BUCKET

The bucket is made of steel and has a toothed edge to help it bite into the ground.

□ BOOM

The boom works as a 3rd class lever. The fulcrum is the hinged joint at the base of the boom (beside the driver's cab), and the load is the dipper arm and the bucketful of soil or rocks.

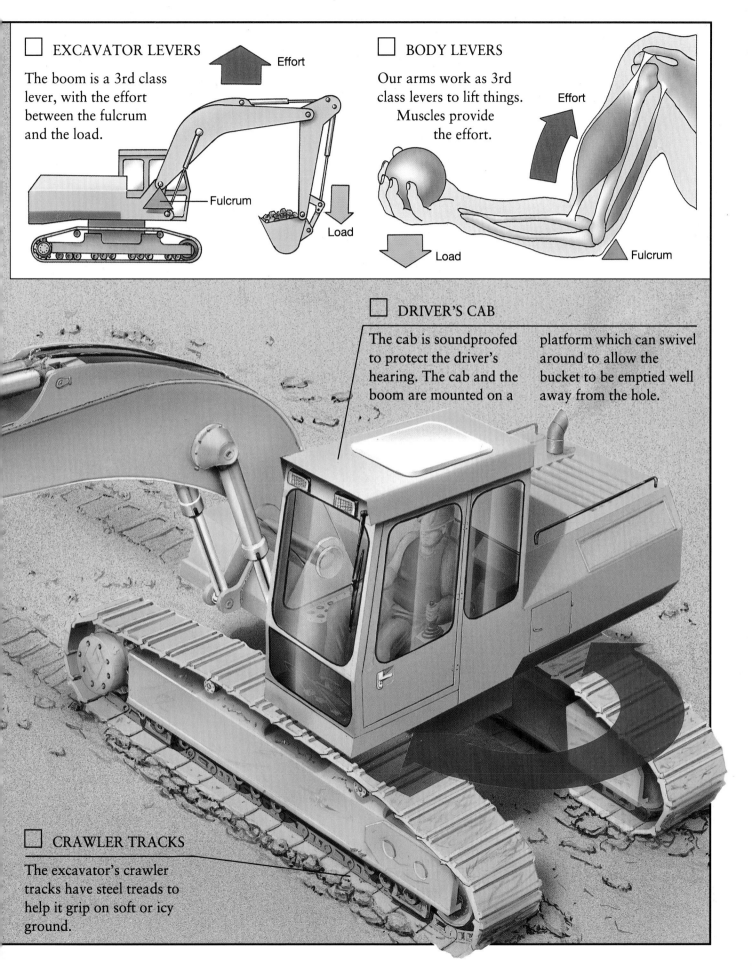

EXCAVATOR LEVERS

The boom is a 3rd class lever, with the effort between the fulcrum and the load.

Effort

Fulcrum

Load

BODY LEVERS

Our arms work as 3rd class levers to lift things. Muscles provide the effort.

Effort

Load

Fulcrum

DRIVER'S CAB

The cab is soundproofed to protect the driver's hearing. The cab and the boom are mounted on a platform which can swivel around to allow the bucket to be emptied well away from the hole.

CRAWLER TRACKS

The excavator's crawler tracks have steel treads to help it grip on soft or icy ground.

FOCUS ON COMPRESSION

One of the big differences between gases and liquids is that gases can be compressed (squeezed) into a smaller space, whereas liquids can't.

Gas   Liquid

Both liquids and gases can send a force through pipes, but liquids are usually used for the heavier tasks.

☐ HYDRAULIC FLUID

The hydraulic fluid used in building machines is a thin oil. Oil doesn't freeze in cold weather, and it keeps the moving parts working smoothly.

PUSHING WITH FLUIDS

The moving parts of many building machines are operated hydraulically. Hydraulic systems use a liquid under pressure to send a force from one end of a pipe to another. If a pipe is connected to a cylinder with a piston inside it, and a liquid is pumped along the pipe into the cylinder, the liquid will push against the piston, forcing it to move. In an excavator, hydraulic fluid is used to push pistons that move the boom, dipper arm, and bucket.

☐ PISTON

The piston is a metal rod with a head that fits tightly inside the cylinder. As the piston slides up and down, it moves part of the building machine.

Piston rod moves up

Piston head

Dipper arm moves down

☐ PUMPING UP

When hydraulic fluid is pumped into the bottom of the cylinder, it pushes the piston up.

Fill an icing syringe with water and push its nozzle into a length of tube. Push the syringe plunger right in, to fill the tube with water (ask a friend to hold the free end up over a sink.) Fill a second syringe with water, taking care not to pull air into the nozzle. Fix the nozzle to the other end of the tube, again trying not to let in any air.

Pushing one plunger in will now force the other one out, because the water sends a force (your push) along the piece of tube.

Plastic icing syringe

Pushes out

Plastic tube (about 8 inches (20 cm) long)

Pushes in

Piston rod moves down

Dipper arm moves up

☐ PUMPING ALONG

Hydraulic fluid is pumped along pipes toward the cylinder. In most building machines, the pumps that push the fluid along are driven by the main engine.

Boom

Bucket

2 PUMPING DOWN

Pumping hydraulic fluid into the top of the cylinder pushes the piston down.

In most building machines, both the brakes and the steering operate hydraulically. Hydraulics are also used in aircraft — for example, to move the landing wheels in and out.

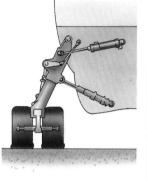

In building machines, hydraulic systems are mainly used to move rams and jacks. A ram is a large cylinder and piston which acts rather like the muscles in an arm, pushing and moving parts of the machine about. Jacks are also large cylinders and pistons, but they work like legs and feet, helping to support and steady machines at work.

☐ BACKHOE LOADER

This machine has two hydraulically operated attachments, one at the front called the front loader, and one at the back called the backhoe.

☐ STABILIZERS

When the backhoe loader is used to do heavy work, hydraulic fluid is pumped along pipes to push out jacks called stabilizers.

These steady the machine and take the weight off the wheels and tires.

Front loader
shovel

Backhoe
bucket
attachment

HYDRAULIC PIPES

Where they need to be able to move with parts of the machine, hydraulic pipes are made of flexible (bendy) material such as rubber. In other places, the pipes are made of metal.

HYDRAULIC RAM

When hydraulic fluid is pumped into the ram, it pushes a piston out. As the piston moves, it makes part of the backhoe move with it.

AT WORK

The backhoe loader is designed to do a wide variety of jobs. Besides digging trenches, these jobs include dozing (pushing soil and rocks out of the way) and grading (making rough ground level).

Digging

Lifting

Grading

Dozing

Grabbing

Loading

Hydraulic pipe

Backhoe

Hydraulic stabilizer

HYDRAULIC HAMMER

This is a special tool which can be fitted in place of the backhoe bucket and used to break up rocks.

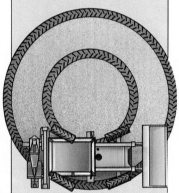

In vehicles with hydraulic steering, fluid is pumped into cylinders, to move pistons in and out. As the diagram below shows, these pistons move the wheels.

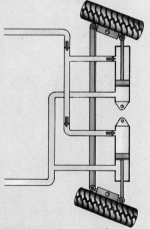

In many cars and trucks, the steering is controlled by a system of rods and gears, not by hydraulic systems.

AT THE CONTROLS

Most building machines have two different kinds of controls. They have driving controls, rather like those in a truck, and they have hydraulic controls to operate rams and jacks. The backhoe loader illustrated below (and on pages 12-13) has attachments front and back, so it has hydraulic controls front and back, as well as a steering wheel and all the other usual driving controls at the front. The backhoe loader's cab has glass all around, and the chair swivels to give the operator a good view whatever the direction of the job.

KEY TO BACKHOE
LOADER CONTROLS

1 Steering wheel
2 Lever for horn, road and indicator lights, and to select forward or reverse driving.
3 Instrument panel—fuel gauge, oil and battery warning lights, etc.
4 Switch for selecting 2- or 4-wheel drive.
5 Windshield wiper switch
6 Gear lever

7 Transmission dump pedal (this works rather like the clutch in a car or a truck).
8 Brake pedals
9 Accelerator pedal
10 Hydraulic control lever for the front loader arm and shovel. Moving the lever back and forward raises and lowers the arms. Moving the lever left rolls the shovel back toward the driver. Moving it right tips the shovel forward to dump the load.

11 Hydraulic control lever for front loader attachments such as a clamshell bucket.
12 Cabin heating
13 Ignition (starter) switch
14 Parking brake
15 Remote boom lock — this holds the backhoe safely against the machine when it is driven on roads.
16 Hydraulic control lever for the backhoe dipper arm and bucket
17 Hydraulic control levers for the stabilizer jacks
18 Hydraulic control for the backhoe boom

DUMPING THE LOAD

Wherever excavators and backhoe loaders are at work digging holes and trenches, there are great piles of rock and soil to clear away. This is a job for dump trucks, and on large construction sites there are usually fleets of them lining up to be filled. The trucks carry the building rubble to dump grounds. Twin hydraulic rams then push up each truck's body to dump the load.

☐ CANOPY

The canopy covers the driver's cab and the engine housing, protecting them from rock spills during loading and dumping.

TEST IT OUT!

Test how high a load has to be raised before it will slip to the ground. You will need something flat and smooth, like the back of a metal tray.

Take the tray outside and load it with a shovelful of soil. Now raise it slowly. How high do you have to lift it before it dumps its load?

☐ WHEELS AND TIRES

Dump trucks need giant wheels with heavy duty tires to provide good grip when hauling heavy loads over soft off-road surfaces.

☐ TRUCK BED

The sloping V-shaped floor of the bed helps to center the load and stop it shifting on hills.

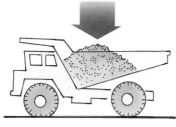

☐ SMALL DUMPERS

Dump trucks come in all sizes. This one can carry about 1.5 tons — it's like a powered wheelbarrow.

☐ ENGINE POWER

Nearly all building machines are powered by diesel engines. These use diesel oil, a heavier fuel than the gasoline used in most cars. Two advantages of diesel engines are that they are more powerful than gasoline engines, and that diesel is cheaper than gasoline. The main difference between the two types of engine is in the way they ignite the fuel.

Diesel engine

☐ HYDRAULIC RAMS

A dump truck's twin hydraulic rams can raise the bed within seconds to dump a load. The giant dump truck shown here can carry a maximum load of nearly 90 tons.

JACKHAMMER AND COMPRESSOR

Air has enormous power, and very many uses, when it is put under pressure by compressing or squeezing it. When used to drive jackhammers, compressed air is strong enough to force a tool through rock or concrete!

Pneumatic or air-driven machines are safer than electrical equipment because they don't produce sparks that could start a fire or cause an explosion. There is also no danger from electric shocks, even when working in wet conditions.

Air filter   Diesel engine   Compression unit

☐ COMPRESSOR

There are three main types of compressor. In one, air is compressed by pistons moving up and down inside cylinders. In the others, air is forced past a spinning turbine or fan, or between two large rotating screws.

Compressed air out

Hose to jackhammer

TEST IT OUT!

Here's a way to see how powerful compressed air is. Take the nozzle off an empty dishwashing liquid bottle and press a small lump of modeling clay into the neck to make it airtight. (If you hold the bottle near your ear and squeeze gently you shouldn't hear any air escaping.)

Take the bottle out-side and lay it on the ground so that it isn't pointing toward anyone. Now jump on the bottle to squash it and compress the air inside. The modeling clay plug will shoot out at great speed, driven by the compressed air!

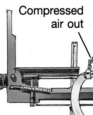

Plug shoots out

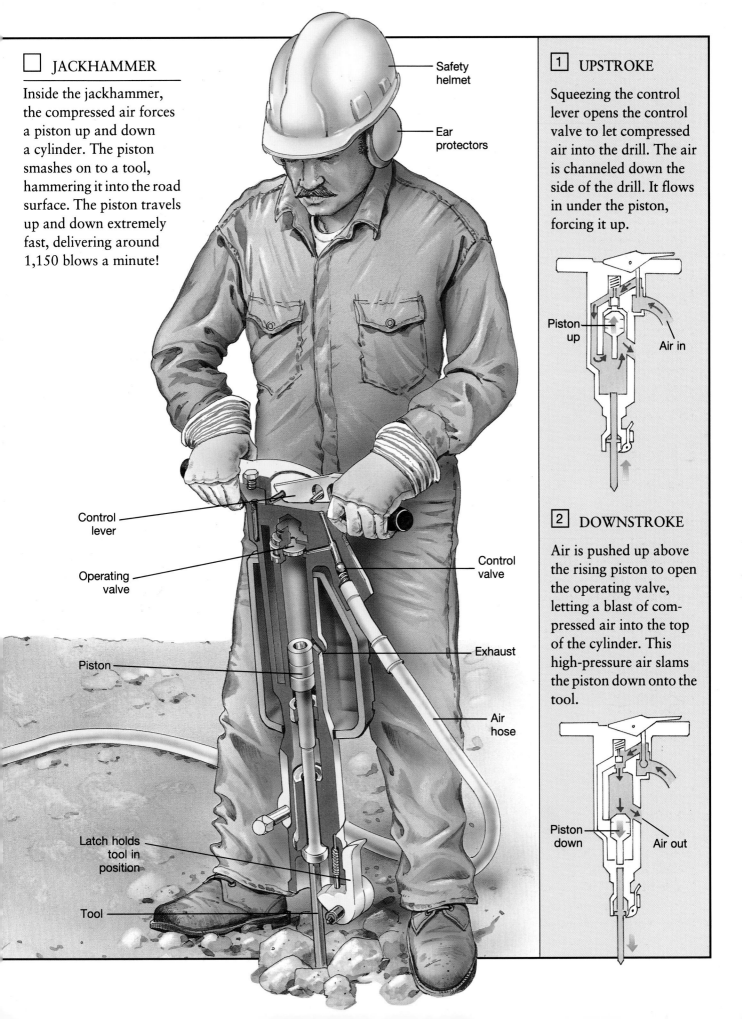

☐ JACKHAMMER

Inside the jackhammer, the compressed air forces a piston up and down a cylinder. The piston smashes on to a tool, hammering it into the road surface. The piston travels up and down extremely fast, delivering around 1,150 blows a minute!

Safety helmet

Ear protectors

Control lever

Operating valve

Control valve

Exhaust

Piston

Air hose

Latch holds tool in position

Tool

1 UPSTROKE

Squeezing the control lever opens the control valve to let compressed air into the drill. The air is channeled down the side of the drill. It flows in under the piston, forcing it up.

Piston up

Air in

2 DOWNSTROKE

Air is pushed up above the rising piston to open the operating valve, letting a blast of compressed air into the top of the cylinder. This high-pressure air slams the piston down onto the tool.

Piston down

Air out

In scientific terms, work is said to be done when an object is moved by a force (a car is moved by a push, for example). The amount of work done is the size of the force multiplied by the distance the object moves. So the same amount of work can either move a heavy object a short distance or a lighter object a lot farther.

☐ REDUCING EFFORT

One person using a double pulley can lift the same weight as two people using a single one. The more pulleys you use, the less the effort needed.

PULLEY POWER

Like levers, pulleys are useful because they make it easier to lift things. A pulley is simply a grooved wheel around which a rope, chain, or cable is passed and tied to something heavy. The object is lifted by pulling down on the other end of the rope. One pulley can be used on its own, or several pulleys can be used together.

☐ SINGLE PULLEY

One pulley doesn't change the amount of effort in a job, but it does change the direction of the effort from a lift to a pull. And it's easier to pull a rope down than to lift something heavy up.

Pulley

Grooved rim
stops tackle
slipping out

Pulley

☐ DOUBLE PULLEY

Two pulleys cut the effort in half, but the rope must be pulled twice as far. More pulleys would cut the effort even further, but the rope would have to be pulled a greater distance.

☐ BLOCK AND TACKLE

Pulleys are mounted in frames called blocks. The rope, chain, or cable is called the tackle.

TEST IT OUT!

To make a single pulley, push some stiff wire through a thread spool and bend the ends round into a triangle. Hang the pulley from a hook. Tie one end of some string to a weight and loop the string over the pulley. How far do you have to pull the string to lift the weight 12 inches (30 cm)?

Unhook your single pulley and thread the string around it, so the wire hangs below the reel. Loop the rest of the string over the top spool.

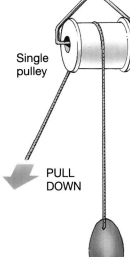

Single
pulley

PULL
DOWN

Double
pulley

PULL
DOWN

Now try a double pulley. Ask a grown-up to nail another spool to a piece of wood. Tie one end of the string to another nail alongside the spool.

Attach the same weight as before to the wire hook below the bottom spool. When you pull the string this time it should be easier to lift the weight. But how far do you now have to pull the string to lift the weight 12 inches (30 cm)?

A square frame is
made much stronger
when it is crossed
diagonally by a brace
or truss. You will often
see braced squares in
the framework of
buildings, as well as
in tower cranes.

**Square is easily pushed
out of shape**

**Braced square is
much stronger**

TOWER CRANE

Cranes are machines that use pulleys to lift and move loads. Different types of crane are designed for different jobs, from loading containers full of goods onto ships, to moving heavy machinery around factories. The tallest cranes in the world are called tower cranes, and they are used to help construct skyscrapers and other tall structures where materials have to be raised to great heights.

☐ CRANE OPERATOR

The operator sits high above the building site in a cab reached by climbing up a ladder inside the framework of the tower.

Trolley
drum

Hoist cable

Operator's
cab

Hoist
drum

☐ COUNTERWEIGHT

The crane's counterweight is made of heavy concrete blocks. It stops the load from pulling the crane over, by balancing the weight of the jib and the load being lifted.

☐ HOIST DRUM

This is driven by an electric motor. When it turns in one direction it winds the hoist cable in, when it turns the other way it lets the cable out.

Climbing
frame

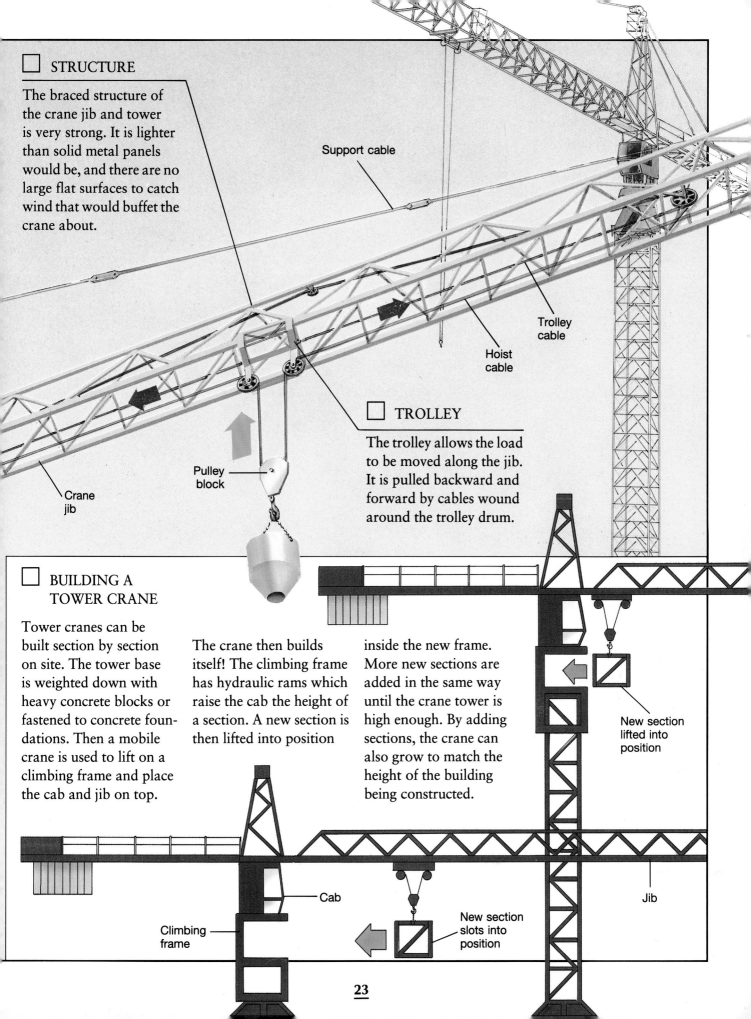

☐ STRUCTURE

The braced structure of the crane jib and tower is very strong. It is lighter than solid metal panels would be, and there are no large flat surfaces to catch wind that would buffet the crane about.

Support cable

Trolley cable

Hoist cable

Crane jib

Pulley block

☐ TROLLEY

The trolley allows the load to be moved along the jib. It is pulled backward and forward by cables wound around the trolley drum.

☐ BUILDING A TOWER CRANE

Tower cranes can be built section by section on site. The tower base is weighted down with heavy concrete blocks or fastened to concrete foundations. Then a mobile crane is used to lift on a climbing frame and place the cab and jib on top.

The crane then builds itself! The climbing frame has hydraulic rams which raise the cab the height of a section. A new section is then lifted into position

inside the new frame. More new sections are added in the same way until the crane tower is high enough. By adding sections, the crane can also grow to match the height of the building being constructed.

New section lifted into position

Cab

Climbing frame

New section slots into position

Jib

FOCUS ON STABILITY

All objects behave as though their whole weight is concentrated in one place. This point is called the object's center of gravity or its balancing point. The lower an object's center of gravity, the more stable it is and therefore the harder it is to tip over.

Counterweights are used to adjust an object's center of gravity and to stop it toppling over.

☐ OUTRIGGERS

Before it can start work, a truck crane has to put down stabilizer jacks to hold it steady and to take the weight off its wheels and tires. Hydraulic rams push out "arms" called outriggers. Then hydraulic jacks are lowered, raising the wheels off the ground.

MOBILE CRANES

Unlike tower cranes, mobile cranes are able to move about under their own power. There are different types. Dockside cranes are usually mounted on rails, for example, so they can travel up and down the length of the dock. Other cranes have crawler treads to spread their weight and help them grip on soft ground. Truck cranes have wheels and tires and can be driven along roads.

The biggest truck cranes are powerful enough to lift about 1,000 tons. Some have telescopic jibs that can extend to over 400 feet (130 m) above the ground. But the higher the jib extends, the less weight it can lift.

☐ COUNTERWEIGHTS

Like tower cranes, truck cranes need counterweights to stop the objects they lift from pulling them over. The truck crane's counterweights are built in, at the base of the jib.

Jib rams

Counterweights built in

Outrigger

Hydraulic jack

☐ TELESCOPIC JIB

The jib is made of sections that fit inside each other, like the sliding tubes of a jointed telescope. The sections slide out hydraulically to make the jib longer.

☐ READY TO ROLL

For journeys between sites, the jib sections slide back inside each other and the jib is lowered. The pulley block clamps on below the cab.

Pulley block

Driver's cab

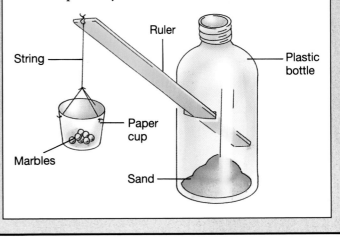

☐ CRAWLER CRANE

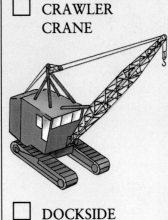

☐ DOCKSIDE CRANE

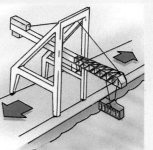

TEST IT OUT!

Here's a way to test how counterweights work. Make a model crane like the one shown below, but without the sand. Will the crane stand up, or does the weight of the bucket pull it over? If it stands up, add marbles to the cup one by one.

How many can you add before the crane falls over? Now pour sand into the bottle to act as a counterweight. How many marbles will the bucket take this time before the crane falls over? Does the sand make it more stable?

Ruler

String

Plastic bottle

Paper cup

Marbles

Sand

A pendulum is a weight (called a bob) that swings from a fixed point. It is stable when the bob hangs directly below the fixed point.

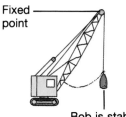

Fixed point

Bob is stable

If the bob is pushed or pulled to one side and then let go, it is pulled back in the opposite direction by the force of gravity.

Gravity makes bob swing

☐ FINE TIMING

One of the earliest uses for the pendulum was in clocks.

WRECKING CRANE

Sometimes old buildings have to be knocked down and cleared away to make way for a road or a new building. Explosives may be used to blow the old building up, or machines may be used to knock it down. Sometimes the wrecking job is done by a mobile crane with a heavy weight attached to it. The weight is swung against the building or dropped down onto it — its smashing force is very effective whichever way it is used!

☐ CRAWLER CRANE

In the crane illustrated here, the jib can be derricked (raised or lowered) to alter its angle. The wrecking ball is attached to two cables. The hoist cable is used to lift and drop it, and the dragline to make it swing.

CRUNCH!

Some of the force of the ball's swing is absorbed as it crashes into the building. This stops the ball swinging back to smash into the crane cab!

Hoist cable

WRECKING BALL

The wrecking ball is made of hardened steel and may weigh several tons. It is pear shaped.

DRAGLINE CABLE

When the dragline cable is winched in, it pulls the wrecking ball with it. When the cable is released, the pendulum effect makes the ball swing toward the building.

TEST IT OUT!

Here's a way to test Galileo's theory about the period of a pendulum. Tie a small weight and a big weight to two equal lengths of string.

Fasten each string to a hook and time ten swings. Both weights should take the same amount of time.

Now repeat the experiment, timing the same weights first with a long piece of string, and then with a short one. You'll find the shorter pendulum swings faster than the long one!

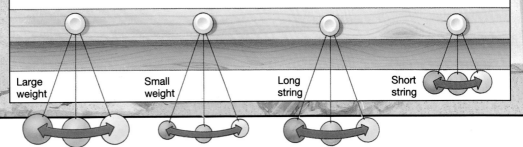

Large weight   Small weight   Long string   Short string

SCREWS AND SCREWDRIVERS

...screwdriver turns,
...force of the turn
passes down to the
screw head. This is
smaller than the screw-
driver handle, so it
turns in a smaller
circle. The difference
in the turning circle
increases the force of
the turn. The screw
pushes into the wood
with greater force than
that used to turn the
screwdriver.

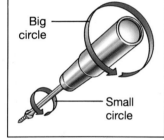

Big
circle

Small
circle

One of the easiest ways of moving a heavy weight is to pull or push it up a ramp, instead of trying to lift it straight up. So, because it makes work easier, a ramp is a simple machine. Surprisingly, screws have ramps in them — the thread of a screw is simply a ramp wrapped around a pole!

Screws have two main uses. One is for fixing and holding things together, and the other is for carrying a load.

☐ THREAD AND PITCH

The thread is the raised or ridged part of the screw. The pitch is the space between the turns of the thread. It is the distance the screw moves in one complete turn.

Screwdriver

☐ WOOD SCREW

Wood screws are used to fix and hold things together. As the screw is turned, its thread pulls it into the wood.

☐ NUT AND BOLT

The inside of the nut has a thread which matches that of the bolt. When the bolt is turned, it screws into the thread of the nut.

Wood
screw

Wrench

Nut

Bolt

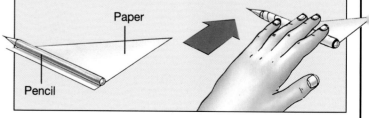

TEST IT OUT!

Here's a way to prove that the thread of a screw is like a ramp. Cut a piece of paper into a ramp shape and wrap it tightly around a pencil. The sloping edge of the paper will spiral around the pencil, just like the thread of a screw.

Paper

Pencil

Drills are tools that bore holes. There are many different types besides construction augers. Small drills are used by dentists to clean away tooth decay, while giant drills are used when boring for oil and natural gas.

CONSTRUCTION AUGER

An auger is a screw with a wide deep thread that can be used to carry a load — for example, lifting soil up out of a hole. A construction auger is used to drill holes to take pipes or foundation piles, so its thread often has a sharp edge to help it cut into the ground.

1 DRILLING DOWN

As the auger drills down into the ground, soil spirals its way upward to fill the deep grooves between the thread.

2 CLEARING THE THREAD

When the auger is full of soil, it is lifted up out of the hole and its thread is cleared. The auger can then be lowered back into the hole to continue drilling into the ground.

CEMENT MIXER

The drum of a cement mixer does two things. When it turns in one direction it mixes the concrete inside it. When it turns in the other direction it works like a device known as an Archimedes screw, to raise the concrete to the mouth of the drum so that it pours down the delivery chute.

Transit truck mixers deliver ready-mixed concrete to building sites. Materials for making concrete are poured into the drum before the truck starts off. Then, as the truck drives along, its drum turns to keep the concrete moving.

Among many important scientific discoveries, the Greek inventor and mathematician Archimedes is thought to have invented a way of raising water from a low level to a higher one by using an auger inside a sloping tube. When the auger's handle is turned, water is "screwed" up the auger's thread.

Handle

Water drawn up auger

☐ ENGINE POWER

Like most trucks, transit truck mixers are powered by diesel engines. The drum is driven either by the main engine or by a separate engine, mounted below the water tank.

TEST IT OUT!

Ask a grown-up to cut the top and bottom off a plastic bottle and help you to wrap and tape about 5 feet (1.5 m) of clear plastic tubing tightly around it. Now hold your Archimedes screw in a bowl of water and turn it very quickly. Water will be drawn up the tube!

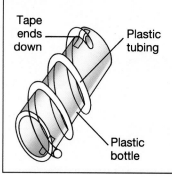

Tape ends down

Plastic tubing

Plastic bottle

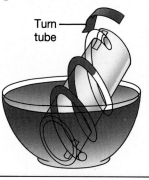

Turn tube

☐ ARCHIMEDES SCREW

Inside the mixer's drum are two spiraling paddles, each one twisted in the opposite direction to the other. Both paddles are fixed to the drum casing and are turned by it. Together, the paddles and drum make a type of Archimedes screw.

☐ LOADING HOPPER

The sand, gravel, and cement to make the concrete are fed into the drum through the loading hopper. Water is added from the tank behind the driver's cab.

☐ MIXING AND POURING

When mixing the concrete, the drum turns in one direction. To raise the concrete so it pours out of the delivery chute, the drum turns in the opposite direction.

Water tank

Delivery chute

☐ POURING THE CONCRETE

When the concrete is ready for pouring, the delivery chute is lowered and swung into position.

The weight of the concrete makes it flow down the chute from the mouth of the drum.

 **FOCUS ON STRUCTURE**

Tunnel walls are curved or arched because a circle is a much stronger shape than a square (unless the square is braced, and you can't brace a tunnel). You can prove this if you make two tunnels — a round one and a square one — from two rectangular pieces of stiff cardboard.

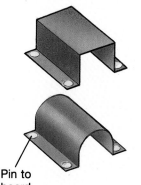

Pin to board

Place coins of the same size on each tunnel, one at a time. The weakest tunnel will collapse first.

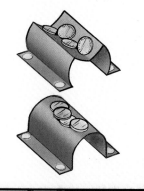

TUNNEL-BORING MACHINE

Tunnel-boring machines (TBMs for short) are used to build large tunnels to carry roads and railroads through mountains and under cities, rivers, and even the sea. They work rather like giant drills, boring their way through the ground. But they can only cut into rocks that are soft and firm, such as chalk, clay, or soft sandstone.

☐ TUNNEL LINING

As the TBM bores forward, huge concrete and metal tunnel lining segments are fitted in position behind it.

☐ TBM OPERATOR

The operator sits in a control cab behind the cutting head. The TBM's systems are monitored by computers. A laser guidance system keeps the machine on course.

☐ HYDRAULIC RAMS

Large powerful rams force the cutting head forward into the rock or soil.

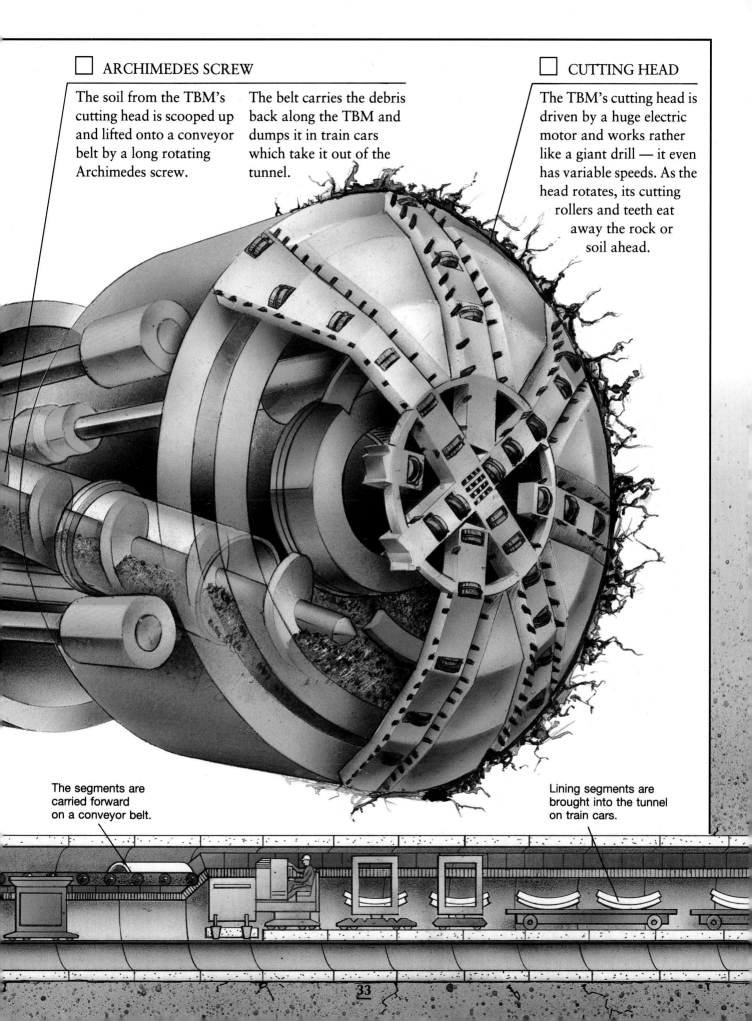

☐ ARCHIMEDES SCREW

The soil from the TBM's cutting head is scooped up and lifted onto a conveyor belt by a long rotating Archimedes screw.

The belt carries the debris back along the TBM and dumps it in train cars which take it out of the tunnel.

☐ CUTTING HEAD

The TBM's cutting head is driven by a huge electric motor and works rather like a giant drill — it even has variable speeds. As the head rotates, its cutting rollers and teeth eat away the rock or soil ahead.

The segments are carried forward on a conveyor belt.

Lining segments are brought into the tunnel on train cars.

FOCUS ON WEIGHT

Bulldozers rarely get bogged in mud even though they are very heavy (the one shown opposite weighs over 11.5 tons). This is because they exert (put out) less pressure on the ground than a full-grown person does. A bulldozer's weight is spread over its long wide crawler tracks, but a person's weight is concentrated on two small feet.

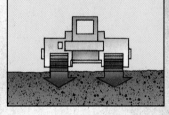

Some of the heaviest construction jobs are done by machines that push and shove. Using strong steel blades they clear sites of rock and soil. Then they shape and level rough ground to take the foundations of bridges, buildings, or roads.

Bulldozers start the ground-preparing work for new roads. Scrapers have a knifelike cutting blade which levels ground by slicing off a layer of soil.

☐ SCRAPER

As the scraper moves forward, its blade slices off a layer of earth and rubble. This is pushed into the bowl by the elevator flights, as they swing past the blade, moving round like escalator stairs.

Elevator flights

☐ SCRAPER BOWL

The trailer part of the scraper is called the bowl. It's made of tough steel and can hold a load of more than 17 tons.

Scraper blade

☐ BULLDOZER

This word was first used in the 1870s. At the time it meant any kind of hard punishment, as in "a dose fit for a bull". It has come to be used for machines since the 1920s. Small machines are sometimes called calfdozers.

☐ SHOVING SNOW

Snowplows keep roads clear of snow. Their blades vary. Single blades are set at an angle so the snow is pushed to one side of the road.

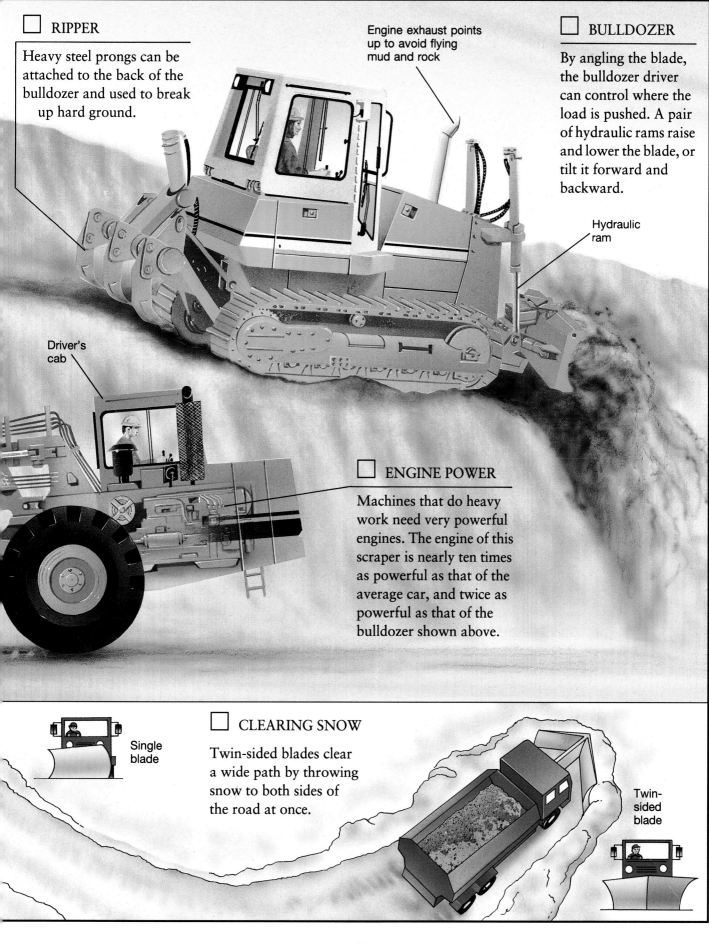

☐ RIPPER

Heavy steel prongs can be attached to the back of the bulldozer and used to break up hard ground.

Engine exhaust points up to avoid flying mud and rock

☐ BULLDOZER

By angling the blade, the bulldozer driver can control where the load is pushed. A pair of hydraulic rams raise and lower the blade, or tilt it forward and backward.

Hydraulic ram

Driver's cab

☐ ENGINE POWER

Machines that do heavy work need very powerful engines. The engine of this scraper is nearly ten times as powerful as that of the average car, and twice as powerful as that of the bulldozer shown above.

Single blade

☐ CLEARING SNOW

Twin-sided blades clear a wide path by throwing snow to both sides of the road at once.

Twin-sided blade

ROAD PAVER

West Indies

South America

Modern roads are made safe and strong by sandwiching layers of different materials together. Most of the layers are put down by machines called road pavers. These are specially designed to lay an even ribbon of road, with none of the bumps that would be a nightmare for fast traffic.

Road paving is a slow and careful job, particularly when laying the surface layers of asphalt. During this stage the road paver crawls along very slowly.

4 SCREED

The asphalt is flattened and smoothed by a heavy attachment called the screed, which fits on to the paver behind the auger. The up-and-down action of tampers and vibrators inside the screed helps to press down the asphalt, but the finishing is mainly done by the soleplate and the weight of the screed.

5 SOLEPLATE

This works rather like a hot iron, to flatten and smooth the asphalt. It is beneath the screed, heated by burners inside it.

Workers make sure the surface is smooth and level

1 HOPPER

Trucks bring steaming hot asphalt from a mixing plant and tip it into the paver's hopper. Flow gates control the rate at which the asphalt is fed on to conveyors.

2 CONVEYORS

Steel conveyor chains run through the paver, carrying the hot asphalt from the hopper to the auger.

THE ROAD SANDWICH

Roads are built up in layers. The rolled and leveled ground on which they are laid is called the sub-grade (1). The sub-base (2) is made of gravel, sand, and a little cement. It supports and drains the layers above it. The road base (3) strengthens the road sandwich by spreading the weight of the traffic evenly. The surfacing (4) is smooth and waterproof. Roads are higher in the middle to help water drain off.

3 AUGER

The asphalt is fed into the thread of the auger. As the auger rotates, it spreads the asphalt. The auger's height and width can be controlled hydraulically.

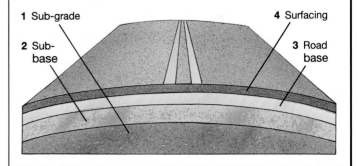

1 Sub-grade
2 Sub-base
4 Surfacing
3 Road base

FOCUS ON VIBRATION

The weight of a steam-roller can smooth a bed of gravel or sand, but vibrations pack it really solid. Vibrations are very fast up and down movements. They get rid of the air pockets that weaken a road, by making sand and gravel jump about until they settle into every available space. This makes the road much more compact and strong.

Before	After

□ ROLLERS

Grass rollers work in exactly the same way as steamrollers. They flatten ground to give a smooth surface for lawn tennis courts.

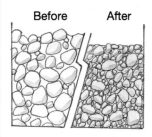

ROLLING AND PACKING

If a road isn't strongly built it will soon begin to break up under the pounding of the thousands of cars and trucks that drive along it. To make a road strong and firm, each of its layers must be flattened until it is hard and smooth. Rolling and packing machines use weight and vibration to do this important job.

□ RAMMER

The "foot" of this hand-held machine vibrates, moving rapidly up and down to flatten narrow strips of sand, gravel, or asphalt. Its packing force is 2,000 pounds (900 kg), which is more than ten times its own weight (when still).

□ SINGLE ROLLER

Rollers come in different sizes, to suit different jobs. This small roller is useful when laying sidewalks or repairing roads. Its drum vibrates as it rolls.

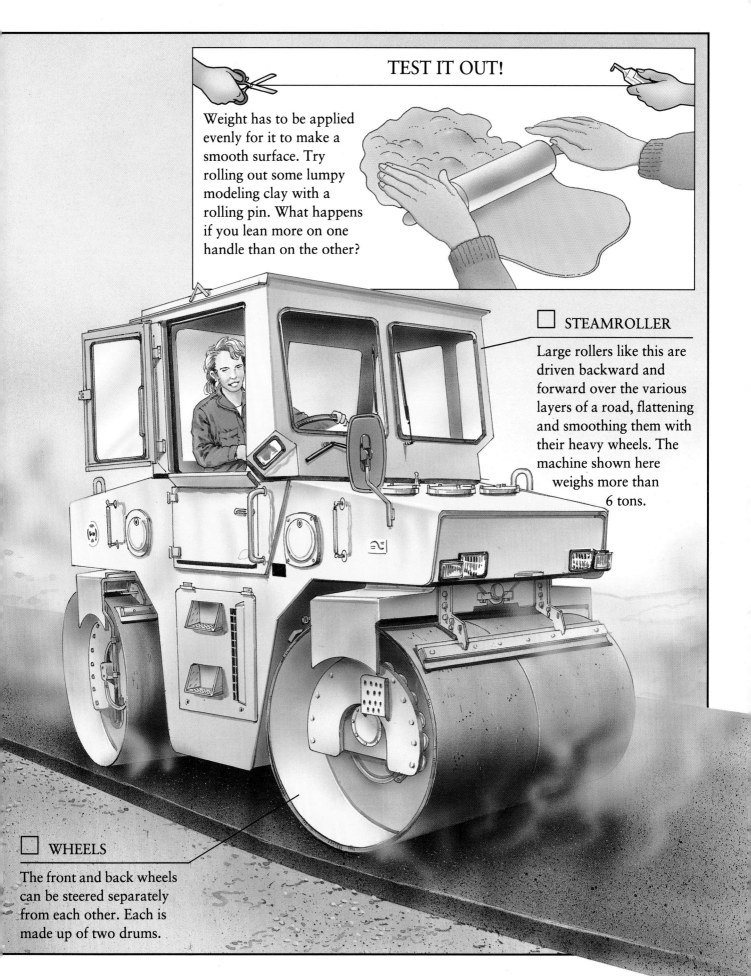

TEST IT OUT!

Weight has to be applied evenly for it to make a smooth surface. Try rolling out some lumpy modeling clay with a rolling pin. What happens if you lean more on one handle than on the other?

☐ STEAMROLLER

Large rollers like this are driven backward and forward over the various layers of a road, flattening and smoothing them with their heavy wheels. The machine shown here weighs more than 6 tons.

☐ WHEELS

The front and back wheels can be steered separately from each other. Each is made up of two drums.

INDEX

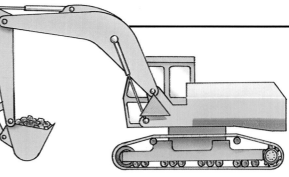

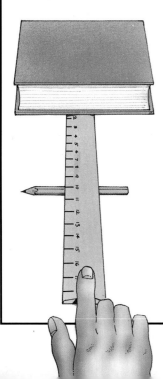